ANGELS TO MY RESCUE
Copyright © 2009 by Roberta Collier

All rights reserved. No part of this book may be reproduced or copied in any form or by any means, electronic, mechanical, photocopying, recording or by any information storage or retrieval system without prior written permission of the Publisher. Inquiries should be addressed to the web address below.

The opinions expressed in this book are those solely of the author and do not reflect the opinions of Million Words Publishing or its Editors.

Unless otherwise noted, all scriptures are from the Holy Bible, NEW INTERNATIONAL VERSION®, NIV® Copyright © 1973, 1978, 1984, 2011 by Biblica, Inc.® Used by permission. All rights reserved worldwide.

Scripture quotations marked (KJV) are taken from KING JAMES VERSION (KJV): public domain.

Thank you.

Published By:
Million Words Publishing, LLC
Enjoyed By You!
WORDS THAT LAST FOREVER!®
www.millionwordspublishing.com

Library of Congress Catalog Card Number:

ISBN #: 978-1-891282-13-3

Angels to My Rescue
Printed in the United States of America

Table of Encounters

Acknowledgements 3-4
Preface 5-7
Introduction 8-10
1 – Mama Said!!! 11-22
2 – Flying on Angels' Wings 23-28
3 – Sweet Smelling Fragrance 29-39
4 – What's A Dude Angel? 40-45
5 – Protected by Man's Best Friend 46-54
6 – Five Shiny Quarters 55-63
7 – A Strange Place for Elevation 64-75
8 – You Gotta Bless Me 76-93
9 – I Was Preparing to Die Until He Spoke
    Life into Me 94-105
I Was Predestined 106-107
About the Author 108-109
Personal Encounter(s) 110

Acknowledgements

Where do I begin . . .?

Thank you, My Heavenly Father, for providing me with spiritual, supernatural resources in the form of angels so that I could share my angelic experiences with others.

Thank you to Dr. Apostle Anthony L. Taylor, Sr. who taught me how to tap into my personally assigned angels that are "encamped around about me" and for teaching the unadulterated Word of God to the New Hope Worship Center body of believers. He continues to give us the gift of life through the preached Word.

I lovingly thank my daughter, LaTonya Collier, and my two grandsons, Jeriah and Darius, Jr., who have encouraged, supported, and respected my walk with Christ. I thank my son Darius, Sr., who has gone on to be with the Lord. He unexpectedly showed me the meaning of God's words, "whosoever will, let him come."

Thanks to my God-given sister, Evone Sims, for being a tireless sounding board on every part of this project, and in many stages of my life.

Last but not least, thanks to the many loved ones who contributed in various ways to writing this book. I could not have done it without any of you.

Preface

Have you ever thought . . . angels . . . are they really real? Have you ever had an experience of assistance or something happen to you or for you that you could not explain, but you knew it happened? Have you physically seen "beings" or "other people" around you that no one else sees? Could it be that you have had full conversations with a person only to find out that person didn't really exist in the natural realm as we know? You have probably heard and perhaps seen many claims from people about experiences where they honestly don't have a clue what to make of them; they just know these experiences are REAL and really did HAPPEN!

During my research about angels, I remembered a well renowned speaker comment on the existence of angels. He commented on our familiarity with UFOs (unidentified flying objects), and then said something very interesting. He also commented on another phenomenon, IFOs, interpreted by him as (identified flying objects) which he called angels. I agree with him because I have had personal encounters with such IFOs.

However, I strongly suggest to you that there is only one absolute and supported source of revealed truth about experiences mentioned above, and that source would be none other than the unadulterated Word of God, which is the Holy Bible. The Bible speaks to the existence of angels in many instances. In my book, the Bible and its history are filled with stories of people who had encounters with angels. Throughout the Scriptures, from Genesis to Revelation, and other reference books, we find accounts of angels visiting people, intervening in their circumstances, advising and informing them, and assisting them in countless ways.

Do not be mistaken that angels and their successful ministering assignments to us and for us, should not take the place, or receive any glory that is due to God the Father and Jesus the Christ. *Angels to My Rescue* simply reminds us of the supernatural assistance God Himself has afforded us through His angels. Upon completion of reading this book, my hope is that we take hold of this spiritual resource and begin using angels for seeking protection, receiving messages from God, deliverance, fighting our battles, and the list goes on. Ponder this: Angels are spiritual beings created by God to serve us here on earth. *"**Are not all angels ministering spirits sent to serve those who will inherit salvation?" Hebrews 1:14**

Introduction

Angels are everywhere doing what they do best—ministering. Angels have been depicted as spiritual beings wearing white apparel, having big wings and living in Heaven with God. That may be true, but if we believe the Word of God, we must believe that angels exist in the spiritual realm. Even though we don't see them often or as we perceive them in the natural, they are spiritual beings that the Lord often sends to earth which can take on whatever form necessary to carry out His will concerning us.

Furthermore, if we could expand our spiritual minds to acknowledge this great resource exists to help us, we can get a lot more accomplished by assigning more to our angels. If you didn't know it, each of God's children has their own guardian angel, just waiting to move on their behalf.

In my book, *Angels to My Rescue*, you will read about some real-life angels that came to my rescue. Some appeared as a messenger in dreams; some served in supernatural acts of deliverance; some as warriors and protectors; and some even visited as strangers unaware. These encounters are supported by scripture, assuring us that God intends for us to access and use the supernatural resources that angels can and will provide. Whatever their assignment, angels are real and a very present help. *"For He will command His angels concerning you, to guard you in all your ways." Psalm 91:11*

Does the thought of "an invisible being" make you cringe or even so, potentially cause the hair on your skin to rise up? Perhaps you might say "I thought I saw something in my peripheral vision, but I turned and saw nothing, or I still feel a presence, it's calming and not scary at all."

One of my favorite passages of scriptures depicting ministering angels is found in *Matthew 4:5-11:*

⁵ Then the devil took him to the holy city and had him stand on the highest point of the temple.
⁶ "If you are the Son of God," he said, "throw yourself down. For it is written: "'He will

command his angels concerning you, and they will lift you up in their hands, so that you will not strike your foot against a stone.'"

[7] *Jesus answered him, "It is also written: 'Do not put the Lord your God to the test.'"*

[8] *Again, the devil took him to a very high mountain and showed him all the kingdoms of the world and their splendor.*

[9] *"All this I will give you," he said, "if you will bow down and worship me."*

[10] *Jesus said to him, "Away from me, Satan! For it is written: 'Worship the Lord your God, and serve him only.'"*

[11] *Then the devil left him, and angels came and attended him.*

After reading *Angels to My Rescue*, my prayer is that you become more comfortable in calling on and recognizing your ministering angels.

Encounter One...
Mama Said!!!

> *"My God sent his angel, and he shut the mouths of the lions. They have not hurt me." Daniel 6:22*

I'd like to begin this encounter by giving a little background of where I lived, and the importance of listening to and obeying what Mama said.

Growing up my family and I lived in a shotgun duplex house in an inner-city neighborhood of North St. Louis. Although we lived in an environment where crime was high, and attracted many undesirables who hid from the law, times were quite different then from how they are now. We knew all of our neighbors, and we also knew most of the frequent visitors, so my family felt safe living there.

We lived on the first floor of the duplex, and our back porch was very dark and only lighted by the kitchen light when our back door was open. As a

Encounter One . . . Mama Said!!!

matter of fact, it was scary if you were on the porch at night and the door was closed because you couldn't see if anyone was hiding there as well.

For those of you who may not be familiar with the term "shotgun house" it simply means you could stand at one end of the house and see straight through to the other end of the house. In our duplex, as in other buildings at that time, there was usually no furnace for heat, so the main heating source was a large, gas soot heater which sat in the middle room of the duplex. Doors surrounding the middle room always had to remain closed to maintain the warmth. The kitchen and the bathroom were located at the back of the house. Listen, I know you are thinking why is it important for me to know this information, please, just stay with me.

One very cold afternoon after I got out of school, I was in the middle room laying across my sister's bed watching the news and I saw a news reporter showing a man who had recently escaped from prison and was loose in the St. Louis area. I paid little attention to what was being said because there was no reason for me to think about it. However, I did remember seeing it. The next day when I got out of school, I again watched TV, but this afternoon I had to go to the bathroom, which as I mentioned was in the back of the house. My mother drilled into our minds (me and my siblings), to always keep the door closed to maintain the heat in the middle room, but for some reason, this time, I did not close the door.

My mother was not home this afternoon and she would always remind us not to open the door for anyone when she was not there. At the time, only my two older sisters and I were home, but they were in the front of the house. Take a listen to what was about to happen within the next 15 minutes.

The encounter starts here . . .

By the time I was out of the bathroom there was a knock at the back door. Before I knew it, I had unlocked the door and whipped it wide open. Then it hit me, I remembered Mama said to never answer the door when she wasn't home, and especially never for strangers. There stood this man that I didn't know, but somehow, he looked eerily recognizable to me. The man immediately stepped inside the house, never closing the door behind him, and he began looking around the kitchen. He then stepped where he could get a closer look straight to the front of the house as if he was looking for somebody or trying to look intently at *something*. As I stood looking at the man, I was terrified because I had opened the door for a stranger and my mama was going to "kill" me. This man reminded me of a dark skinned Native American (maybe a mix of African American and of Indian descent). He looked to be about 5'8 or 5'9 in stature and had a medium body build. He didn't have on a jacket, which was odd because it was cold out, but he did have on an orange shirt. I managed to utter to the stranger, "Do you know us?" The stranger never really looked at me nor did he answer me. *Something* had his attention up front.

As the stranger stood looking from the back of the house straight through to the front, suddenly, he asked me in broken English, "Is that big guy in there your daddy?" I stood dumbfounded beside him because I knew there was no man in there, and from where I was standing, I didn't see one either. It certainly wasn't my father because he had died when I was two years old. I was around 12 at this time, so I did not understand what was happening or what the stranger was seeing. I reluctantly answered the stranger, "No, that's not my father." He asked me, "Do you have a big brother?" I said, "Yes."

I did have a big brother; however, my brother was not home either. Immediately the stranger looked as if he had seen a ghost and he turned to run out of the open door. As he turned to run, I noticed a knife in his hand which had a sharp serrated blade on it, at least it looked sharp. At the time I didn't really know what to make of this incident. After all, I had never personally witnessed such a thing even though I did live in a "rough" neighborhood.

Who or what did the stranger see? How big was this man that he saw which made him think he was seeing either a daddy figure or a big brother? Why was he troubled by seeing the man so much so that he turned and ran without completing any type of act? Apparently, this guy was a very big-statured man that left the stranger visibly shaken. Who was this big man and where did he go? After the stranger left and I locked the door, I was really scared, but I decided not to tell anyone what had just happened. I saw that knife in the stranger's hand over and over in my mind and could only be grateful unto God for saving my sisters and me.

I kept hearing in my mind the voice of my mother's commandment of never opening the door for strangers. What was I thinking? I knew if I told my sisters, they would tell Mama and she would have killed me for sure, meaning I would have gotten a really bad "whooping."

I thought about that incident for a couple of days, and as repetition would have it, I was watching the news and the reporter mentioned again that a man had broken out of jail, and he was still on the loose, and that he was armed and dangerous. I sat straight up on the bed and my teeth began to chatter from what I saw. **THAT MAN** on TV was the same man that appeared at our door a couple of days earlier. The **SAME MAN** I had let into our house. Terror, panic, and fear went through my young body and heart. But I never said a word to anyone, at least not until now.

I know now what the stranger would have done if my protector wasn't there. There were no lions there, but that day the mouth of evil was shut, and my sisters and I were not harmed. *"My God sent his angel, and he shut the mouths of the lions. They have not hurt me." Daniel 6:22* Hallelujah!!!

God revealed to me the multitude of protection given on that day and even in my young, inexperienced mind, God was unfolding to me my first encounter with the "angel world." He revealed to me that I had His protection then, and that the "big brother" or "father figure" that the man had seen, was just an "Angel to My Rescue." Back then I didn't know clearly what was on the mind of this intruder, but today I am fully aware and know all too well, "But God! Hallelujah for my Angel!!!"

PONDER THIS

Apostle Paul said, *"When I was a child, I spoke as a child, I understood as a child, I thought as a child: but when I became a man, I put away childish things." 1 Corinthians 13:11 (KJV)* A child is sometimes a little disobedient, curious, and will do things that they should not do. I was young when this encounter happened, and I should not have opened the door to the stranger, nor should I have left the middle door opened. After all, these were things "Mama said" not to do. Somehow, the "open doors" provided an opportunity for the angel to be seen by the perpetrator. Most "open doors" are opportunities to provide us with a way into something, or a way out of something. Either way, movement is involved when an open door is before you. God makes a way of escape for us from seen and unseen dangers through open doors. He causes our worlds to shake both literally and figuratively when he is delivering us from bondage, danger, or an unfortunate situation.

I am reminded of the open door experience that the Apostle Paul and his friend, Silas, experienced in the Roman prison.

CHECK THIS OUT:

²²"The crowd joined in the attack against Paul and Silas, and the magistrates ordered them to be stripped and beaten with rods. ²³After they had been severely flogged, they were thrown into prison, and the jailer was commanded to guard them carefully. ²⁴When he received these orders, he put them in the inner cell and fastened their feet in the stocks. ²⁵About midnight Paul and Silas were praying and singing hymns to God, and the other prisoners were listening to them. ²⁶Suddenly there was such a violent earthquake that the foundations of the prison were shaken. At once all the prison doors flew open, and everyone's chains came loose. ²⁷The jailer woke up, and when he saw the prison doors open, he drew his sword and was about to kill himself because he thought the prisoners had escaped." Acts 16:22-27

The open doors here represented an awesome, impossible, and powerful experience that no man could do alone! But with God, open doors are what He does! Hallelujah!!!

Encounter One . . . Mama Said!!!

Some may say my sisters and I were just lucky. I say luck had nothing to do with it. God is the only one who knows how to take a bad situation and turn it around for our good. Look at Daniel 6:16, ***"So the king gave the order, and they brought Daniel and threw him into the lions' den. The king said to Daniel, "May your God, whom you serve continually rescue you!"'*** When King Darius' hands were tied, God stepped right in and sent Daniel's angel to the rescue. God did just what the King hoped He would do, rescue Daniel! We do not worship angels above God in any way, nor do we share God's glory with them, but we do thank God for the resource of ministering angels. Of a truth, had it not been for the angel that God sent for me and my sisters, who knows what the outcome might have been. God blessed me and kept me because He knew He had a plan and a future for me. Hallelujah!!!

Don't be fooled! Angels still exist today, and they are a present help when we find ourselves in less than favorable and safe atmospheres. Remember that God is not going to put you in danger, or if you do find yourself in a situation as did Daniel when he was in the lion's den, God will provide you a way of escape. God sent his angel to close the mouth of the hungry lions and Daniel was able to rest with the lions and not worry about being eaten. God gives each of us who trust in Him at least one guardian angel to serve on our behalf, and it is up to us to use this resource by giving assignments. Assignments of protection are a good place to start with your angel. Please read Daniel, Chapter 6, and receive some encouragement in trusting God and using the resources He affords us.

When we learn more about using the supernatural resources God gives us, it catapults us into having attitudes of being more than conquerors in our walk with Christ Jesus. Thank God for His angels of protection.

PRAYER

Lord, thank you for the angel(s) you have encamped around about me and I ask you to send my angel(s) to protect my going out and my coming in. Protect my children as they go to and from school.

Encounter One . . . Mama Said!!!

Stand at the doors of my home and keep evil from harming us. Lord, when I am in the "lion's den" or places that may not seem favorable for me, I ask that the angel(s) shuts the mouth of the lions so that I may accomplish whatever Your will may be. I realize that there is nothing that can happen to me each day that together You and I can't handle! I thank you for my ministering angel(s). In Jesus' mighty name. Amen

Encounter Two...
Flying on Angels' Wings

> *"Bless the LORD, ye His angels, that excel in strength, that do His commandments, hearkening unto the voice of His word." Psalm 103:19-21*

During this encounter I worked as a Telecommunications Manager for our local phone company. One night I worked late preparing seminar material for an upcoming corporate policy seminar. I was extremely tired because I had begun my workday at six o'clock that morning, and left work about ten thirty that evening. My office was in a prestigious hotel in West St. Louis County.

My daily commute was approximately 20 miles each way on Highway 70 unless I had a detour to make. This particular night was detour-free; however, I must admit I was very tired. What happened next befuddles me even to this day. I must have either dozed off unknowingly for a few seconds, or I was driving asleep, or I was looking down at something. To be very honest, I don't really know what happened because as I said **I WAS VERY TIRED!!!**

At some point I noticed I was driving about 65 miles per hour and when I looked up and focused on what was happening in front of me, it seemed as if the highway traffic had been hidden to me because the next thing I knew I was about three or four car lengths away from a highway full of red brake lights in standing still traffic. Oh my God!!! What!!! There was no time to stop!!! I was driving too fast!!! I immediately took my foot off the gas pedal and put my foot on the brake pedal. Out of instinct, I called on the name of Jesus three times, JESUS! JESUS! JESUS! I took both hands off the steering wheel and put my hands up to my face because I knew I was getting ready to crash into the already sitting sea of traffic in front of me.

I forgot to mention that I was in the left-hand driving lane next to the dividing wall of opposite traffic, so I could not maneuver to another lane. All of this was happening so fast. In my mind's eye the final few seconds of my life played out the horrible way one would think it would in this inevitable accident situation. But, what, what is that terrifically loud sound that sounds like the mighty wings of a huge bird or something with wings? **SWOOSH! SWOOSH! SWOOSH! SWOOSH! SWOOSH**! I heard this sound at least five times.

When I hesitantly took my hands away from my face to see why I had not crashed already into the back of the cars ahead of me, and to see where that loud noise was coming from, I noticed I was no longer in the left driving lane, but I was in the right hand lane of the highway exiting off at Lucas and Hunt Road. How could that happen? What just happened? One minute I was getting ready to run into a sea of sitting traffic with no doubt that I would have been killed and possibly killing or badly injuring many others in the left-hand lane, but I miraculously ended up in the farthest right lane exiting off of the highway! Go figure! I mean for real for real!!!

I drove the remainder of the way home totally in a daze and truly grateful again to God for saving my life.

Encounter Two . . . Flying on Angels' Wings

Tears were rolling down my face and I was screaming to the top of my lungs, **THANK YOU JESUS FOR SAVING ME!!!** Although I never saw the Angel, nobody had to tell me that there was an Angel!! I heard his mighty wings of strength and rescue.

This is just me saying, apparently, the ministering angel had to pick my car up and sit it in the exit lane. I wonder if anyone saw this in the natural world. How else could I have gotten to the exit lane, because I certainly did not do it myself? You had to be there to see there was no time to stop. I was three lanes over from the exit lane, and there were cars in each of those lanes already. How did my life get spared through this natural impossibility that I will never be able to prove? What I do know is that I thanked God every day for a very long time for another encounter with my Angel to My Rescue.

PONDER THIS

Angels have supernatural strength and power given to them by God. You may have heard others talk about those that gain supernatural power to lift cars and other things when it came to the rescue of their loved ones from danger. That is truly amazing in itself. But to lift a whole car and place it three lanes over without anyone being hurt, that is nothing short of miraculous!

Revelation 18:21 reads, "Then a mighty angel took up a stone like a great millstone and threw it into the sea." This gives us another account of how strong angels are while doing the work of the Lord.

In researching various resources to find out the weight of a "great millstone" it is said one millstone could weigh upwards to 3500 pounds. Many of us are very familiar with the strength of men who may be able to pick up many heavy things, and can pull buses, but who are no match against one of God's mighty angels.

I know that I am not the only one who has miraculously been saved from a horrific tragedy. Angels are more than magical beings that fly around in white robes with huge wings. I believe at God's command; they serve and minister to us when we need them.

Encounter Two . . . Flying on Angels' Wings

PRAYER

Lord, I thank you for being Jehovah, the one who is my protector!!! Thank You for being a miracle worker in the time of need. Who wouldn't serve a God like You!!! Help me God to continually look to the hills from whence cometh my help, because truly, all of my help comes from You. Help me to hear You when You tell me to go right, and don't let me go left. Help me to hear Your voice and know when You are speaking to me. I realize and know that obedience is better than sacrifice, so help me not to take shortcuts to save time, or because it may seem less complicated, but help me to be obedient and seek Your direction for me. Thank You, Lord, for the ministering angels You have commanded to be of assistance to me. I will be careful to give You all the glory, the honor, and praise just for who You are. I love You Lord; I thank You and I glorify Your name. Amen.

Encounter Three...
Sweet Smelling Fragrance

> *"Walk in love, even as Christ also loved you, and gave himself up for us, an offering and a sacrifice to God for a sweet-smelling fragrance." Ephesians 5:2*

Around March 2008, I coordinated and conducted a marriage retreat that was held in an exclusive hotel in Central Missouri for some couples at my church, New Hope Worship Center. There was no part of this retreat that I did not acknowledge my Father for instructions. For every step of planning and preparation I invited God to be the strategist and asked Jesus to help me offer a project that God the Father would approve.

Of course, after much prayer, many days of detailed planning, and an eagerness to get things going, the days of execution were at hand. The retreat was a three-day, all-inclusive event where each day had its own purpose and agenda. Now, I must tell you,

Encounter Three . . . Sweet Smelling Fragrance

even with the best planning of details, things don't always turn out as planned. The couple who was going to teach the "ministering" portions of the retreat called and canceled three days before the retreat!!! They had an offer to speak at a conference in Africa. I think I would have gone to Africa as well if I had been given that opportunity! Oh well, that didn't help me at all, and I wasn't able to find anyone on such a short notice.

Not only that, upon arriving at the resort, I realized I had left the entire bag of "eats" for that evening on the counter at my house. There were segments that I was to facilitate, and yes, guess what, my notes were lost. I could not find them anywhere, even though I know I put them in the car with other paperwork. OMG!!! I was a mess!!! These mishaps were only the beginning of a list of things where I had to be a great improviser.

On to the encounter at hand. At the end of the retreat I had arranged a Vow Renewal Ceremony and a reception to celebrate the couples and their achievements. I had made arrangements with the Sales & Catering Staff for room rental that included the necessary tables and chairs only, because I had brought everything else I needed to make this a special event for the couples.

Upon arrival, the room was more beautiful than I could have expected. Everywhere you looked, you could see the room was adorned in beautiful cherry wood. While bringing in the supplies, I was greeted by an older lady and a young boy about 11 or 12, maybe a little older. Although they were not dressed in typical hotel attire (black and white), they welcomed me to the hotel and introduced themselves to me (I don't remember their names now), and I in turn did the same. The lady was carrying a spray bottle in her hand full of liquid and the lad was standing behind her. I asked what they did for the hotel and she told me her job was to present a "sweet smell" before the entrance of their special guests. I thought that was very different, but told her that's a nice addition from the welcoming committee. She began to spray the carpet and it really did have a sweet-smelling aroma. While we were working, they left but came back. Chef Shawn, who was with me at the time, had a question to

Encounter Three... Sweet Smelling Fragrance

ask, and the lady volunteered to go and get someone who could help us.

I had already been told by the Sales & Catering Staff that they didn't have any events going on that weekend so no staff would be available to assist us since we were only renting the room without setup assistance. But, a few minutes later, a young woman in a white shirt and black pants (typical hotel attire) arrived and asked us how she could help us. Chef Shawn asked for the item he needed, and she asked if that was all that we needed. Well, I thought if we could get three linen tablecloths that would be great. She said she would bring the tablecloths and I thought perhaps I could get tableware, since she was offering, instead of the paper products I had brought. The room was so beautiful and now my paper products didn't seem to fit with the ambience. To make a long story short, she provided tableware and linen napkins for about 30 people! Wow, I thought that was unbelievably kind and customer oriented! Once she brought all the items to us, she bid us a good night and told us to put the used dishes on the carts she provided in the room across from us.

After everything was set up and the room looked absolutely beautiful, the lady and lad came back in and sprayed one more time and she reiterated that her job was to usher in a sweet-smelling aroma for those to come. I asked her if she knew any staff member that we could borrow a CD player from. She brought back this player from someone in the hotel and I thanked her and continued to complete last minute details.

When the Chef was preparing his food and wrapping it for transport from the resort to the hotel, he told me that something had instructed him to double, and triple wrap all the food, so he did. When he was loading the cart to bring in the food, the cart was on a slight incline and somehow got away from him and rolled down the incline, fell over and all the food fell off the cart. He immediately leveled the cart and reloaded everything back on the cart. Guess what, not one thing wasted out of any of the food trays, all because he had gotten that extra "inner" instruction to wrap everything very well.

Encounter Three . . . Sweet Smelling Fragrance

After the ceremony (which was very successful by the way), we cleaned the room and removed all the dishes as promised. Then I went to the Front Desk to ask if they knew how I could locate the lady and lad who greeted us earlier, and the young lady from Sales & Catering. I began to tell the Front Desk Attendant how graciously they helped us to enjoy a beautiful reception. I wanted to tip them and personally thank them for the services they provided us. The Front Desk Attendant asked me what these people did for me and I told her the lady and the lad had welcomed us to the hotel and told me their job was to provide a sweet-smelling aroma for their guests. The attendant asked me to describe them and I did. She told me their hotel did not employ such people. I began to explain to her again how the lady was spraying a sweet-smelling liquid and she was instrumental in obtaining help from the Sales & Catering Staff, the young lady who allowed us to use the tableware. She said that was impossible because they didn't have any events for that weekend besides us, and we were only using the room and no setup staff was needed. She checked her book and told me again, "There is no one on the clock who would have done that." Now come on, how could we see with our own eyes, people who assisted us and then be told they didn't exist or work in that hotel?

So, a few days after I arrived back in St. Louis, I contacted the Sales Manager to tell her how wonderful her staff was who provided us with tableware and linen napkins for about 30 people. She was not a happy camper and thought I had taken advantage of the situation because there was not supposed to be any staff on duty that weekend. However, the dishes were there to prove SOMEBODY gave them to us. We could not have gotten the dishes on our own because we didn't know where to get them from! I started wondering myself: 1. Who were those people? 2. How could they meet our every need not having worked there? And 3. Where did they disappear to? Well, it didn't matter if the Sales Manager believed me or not-it happened!

Prior to the end of this entire event, I was truly "bumming" because very little had gone the way I planned and that was not good in my eyesight. And

Encounter Three... Sweet Smelling Fragrance

wouldn't you know it, my notes that I could not find in order to complete my portion of the retreat were hidden right in front of my eyes. I found them, after the ceremony, laying in plain view on the counter in my condo at the resort. I used that counter each of those three days I was there. How did I not see them? Well, I did ask God to be the strategist and asked Jesus to help me to carry out an event that God approved of. I am guessing that was just what God had strategized because most of the couples raved and told me that they had such a great time at this marriage retreat! Thank you again for my "Angels to My Rescue!"

PONDER THIS

Even though the "angelic" existence for this experience was centered around the appearance of these two people who served as angels, or the very appearance of angels serving as these two people, I could not go any further without pointing out the real focal point of how much Jesus loves us. Jesus loves us so much that His life is the greatest example of love and sacrifice, so much so, that He pleased God, and it was to God a "sweet smelling fragrance."

Jesus cares about everything that concerns us, in that, He showed up for this conference. He showed up for every couple seeking healing in their marriage. He provided "angels" (in the form of the lady and the lad), whose only job was to provide us with a sweet-smelling fragrance. Now, I can't explain where the lady, the lad, and other staff came from, but what I do know is that they answered ALL our needs and wants when it came to the complete setup of this conference. That's just like Jesus; does He not step up and handle the situation better for us than we could have ever even thought to ask for?

I had a detailed agenda planned and thought surely that's what God had given me. But as it turned out, He wanted each couple to share with their spouses memories of the things that made them fall in love in the first place. We were at a beautiful condo overlooking the lake and the atmosphere was set for everyone to enjoy themselves which is what God wanted for the couples. Also, when it was time to

Encounter Three . . . Sweet Smelling Fragrance

deliver a Word from God, my Pastor stepped right in with an on-time message.

This experience was not a life threatening or need for protection against evil, but just a sincere desire for God to show up and be a part of these marriages in a mighty way by meeting the needs of these couples through healing, giving understanding, and restoring love. I fasted and prayed earnestly for God's presence and direction. Because of God's love for me and each couple attending this retreat, little did I recognize, God was already many steps ahead of me and had the plans for each couple already worked out.

PRAYER

Father, I thank You for knowing me inside and out. You know everything there is to know about me. You know how I think, how I feel, what's better for me, and You have prearranged plans that will work for me. Jeremiah 29:11 tells me that God knows the plans He has for each of us. Help us to accept and know the plans You have for us won't harm us but that You have a promise for our lives regardless of our present situation. We know our best isn't enough sometimes and that's when You step in. Help me to purpose in my heart to rest in knowing You will work through whatever I am going through, You will prosper me, and give me hope. Thank You, Lord, for who You are to me!!! Amen.

Encounter Four...
What's A Dude Angel?

> *"O Lord, please open his eyes that he may see. So the Lord opened the eyes of the young man and He saw horses and chariots of fire all around Elisha."*
> *2 Kings 6:17*

One summer night, about 11 pm, I left my home to go and pick my brother up from work. On our way back home to our neighborhood in North St. Louis City, we stopped at a service station. If you happen to know anything about this neighborhood, you wouldn't want to be out at 11 pm. However, I had lived there for a few years and felt safer than a stranger would.

Anyway, my brother got out of the car to go and pay for gas while I waited in the car. As I sat there, I saw in my side mirror, a man approaching my car. As he neared my window, I saw he was a tall, nice looking man. What was I thinking, or was I thinking at

Encounter Four . . . . What's A Dude Angel?

all? Duh, it was almost midnight and no good thing happened at midnight in this area of North St. Louis City!!!

At any rate, he walked up to the car and started flirting with me. He asked me what a pretty thing like me was doing out this time of night by myself and he made a few more small talk comments. I told him I wasn't by myself, but I was waiting on my brother to come and pump gas into the car. He looked towards the direction of where my brother was standing on the outside of the pay station because the inside was closed. He asked, "Which one of those dudes is your brother?" Well, now, I looked in that same direction and I only saw ONE man, which was my brother. I responded, "Yes, that one is my brother." He asked, "Is he with those two big dudes standing next to him?"

So, as I mentioned, I didn't see anyone standing by my brother. However, the man described "those two big dudes" as if they were bigger than the average man. So, you ask, what is a "dude angel?" Well, you won't find the phrase "dude angel" in the Bible; so, you don't have to look for it. But, in my mind's eye, I would tell you my "dude angels" were those two big, strong, and valiant beings standing by my side, and my brother's side at that time, waiting and watching to protect, to be a warrior, or just plain ready to take on the battle for God's children! I praise God for my "dude angels."

By this time my brother was walking towards the car, and I assumed those two "big dudes" were walking with him, because Mr. Handsome took off running without getting my number or telling me bye. I can't say for sure what could have happened, but I could have been carjacked, kidnapped, robbed, and only God knows what else. My thinking is this, if there was no danger to be had for my brother or myself, there would not have been a need for the "dude angels" to appear. God, however, didn't see fit for any kind of danger to occur. THANK YOU, JESUS!!!

At this stage in my life, my encounters with angels were becoming more frequent and because of what just happened all I could say was thank you Lord, Jehovah-Sabaoth, The Lord of Hosts, and our Protector, for my "Angels to My Rescue."

Encounter Four... What's A Dude Angel?

PONDER THIS

When the average person thinks about the appearance of an angel, our minds immediately go to a human-looking character in a white robe with wings. Or, perhaps we think of a cute little chubby cherub kneeling and looking so innocent. In 2 Kings 6:17, when the young servant informed Elisha that they were outnumbered by the enemy and were going to lose the battle, Elisha prayed that his servant's eyes be opened to see the many horses and chariots of fire which God had sent in the form of a host of angels, powerful, mighty beings that surrounded them. God doesn't leave us to fight our seen or unseen battles alone.

As a matter of fact, He doesn't instruct us to fight, but one fight. What fight is that, you say? According to 1 Timothy 6:12, God tells us to fight the good fight of faith. I know some of my brothers and sisters are saying they are fighting on the battlefield of the Lord everyday as they sing the song, "I'm on the Battlefield for My Lord," and sings it with fervor. But fighting the good fight of faith requires God to open your spiritual (and sometimes natural) eyes, to allow you to see what you are really fighting in faith with.

For instance, when you are fighting the spirit of lack or poverty, God has to open those spiritual eyes so that you can see that you walk in the shoes of the lender and not the borrower! Or, when the adversary tries to make you think you are not worthy of that promotion or owning your own business, again God has to show you that you are the head and not the tail—you can do it! Maybe when you are fighting with sickness and disease and the enemy is telling you that you are going to die, God steps up and opens your eyes and shows you the faith fight which tells you to confess that you shall live and not die! Do you not know those things that are invisible are more real than those things you actually see with your natural eyes? Lord God, please open our eyes that we may see the chariots of fire and thousands of angels waiting to fight on our behalf.

When the "dude" angels showed up for me that night, God opened the eyes of the flirtatious man to let him know this is a battle you won't win, a battle you can't win, I GOT HER!!! When God opens our spiritual eyes and gives us a glimpse of His plans for us, our hearts are enlightened and encouraged because He has our back. We are then able to stand flat-footed and toe-to-toe with the enemy (in faith) and let him know that no weapon he has formed against us shall prosper.

PRAYER

Thank You, Lord, for eye-opening faith that will cause me to move mountains and to slay giants, realizing that giants do fall with You in the driver's seat. Help us to walk by faith in everything we do so that we can be confident disciples for You. Help us to walk in Your spiritual guidance so that our inner man is strengthened and renewed daily. There are no surprises in You, so we thank You for sending our angels before us. Thank You for loving us the way You do! In Jesus' name. Amen.

Encounter Five...
Protected by Man's Best Friend

> *"Then he continued, "Do not be afraid, Daniel. Since the first day that you set your mind to gain understanding and to humble yourself before your God, your words were heard, and I have come in response to them." Daniel 10:12*

So, one morning as I prepared for my normal, outstanding day with the Lord as my guide, I left my house to go and catch the local transportation because I didn't have a car at this time. Because I knew my surroundings were not the safest, every morning before I left, I sought God for my safe arrival to my destination. As I locked my door, I turned to my right to walk to the bus stop which was roughly two blocks away.

Encounter Five . . . Protected by Man's Best Friend

Have you ever felt that someone was following you, or in your presence, but you couldn't see them; you could only feel them? Well, I was having one of those moments on this day. As I was walking, I happened to look to my left looking somewhat over my shoulder and I spotted this stray dog walking behind me. Where did he come from? I was walking very cautiously and never saw him until that moment. My heart skipped ten beats instead of two beats—nine beats because I was terrified of dogs because they have teeth, and have a tendency to bite people who seem afraid, and one beat because the dog caught me totally off guard.

Yes, I know that saints aren't supposed to be afraid, but at that moment, I was "scurred" not scared, and fear was holding on. As I got closer to the bus stop which was across the street, I could see no one else standing there, as usual. It was about 6:30 am and still dark. The bus was due at 6:43 am. Anyway, I did not have a stick and that dog had gotten in front of me and was standing in my path looking at me. Man, what was I to do? I couldn't go back home, the bus was due in minutes, so I stood there and asked God to make a way for the dog to leave.

The dog stared at me for what seemed like a minute and then darted into this vacant building on the same side of the street. Woo! This was my opportunity to cross the street because the bus stop was on the other side of the street. So, I began to speed my walk because the bus should have been on its way by now. However, as I was crossing the street, what did I see, but that dog standing at the corner. The bus was coming and I had no choice but to keep crossing the street and get on the bus as it pulled up. With my chest in my throat, I walked quickly past the dog, got on the bus, and sat on the bus centering myself in thankful prayers and reminded myself of the outstanding day the Lord and I had planned.

The next day I got up and completed my usual morning routine including asking God's protection over me and others as we go about our daily lives. When I walked out of the door to catch my bus, of course, I looked around to see if that dog was anywhere near. However, I did not see it. So, I went

Encounter Five . . . Protected by Man's Best Friend

down the street humming and singing to myself as I usually do and halfway to the bus stop, who or what did I see? Yes, you guessed it, "that dog!!!" Yesterday's activity was relived, and I asked the Lord once again to remove the dog so that I wouldn't miss my bus. Once again, the dog went into the vacant building, I crossed the street and yes, the dog met me at the bus stop. I stood looking at the dog and the dog stood looking at me.

After I safely boarded the bus, and was centering myself for the day, I began to ask God to reeeeeeeally move the dog from my path in the mornings because I was afraid of him. I felt he was going to make me miss my bus, and maybe even attack me since I know he sensed my fear. It was at that point that God revealed to me my answered prayer. Every morning when I prayed, I would ask God for traveling mercies for me and others. Wouldn't you know it; this dog was my traveling mercy!!! Hallelujah!!!

So, day three the dog met me and without praying for him to leave, he did anyway. Although, this time I didn't need for him to leave because I knew his purpose for that moment and that was to protect me. When I got to the corner, who did I see but "that dog." In the days past I may have dreaded tremendously seeing him, but now I am looking for him, and there he was at the bus stop waiting for me. Yeah!!!

This interaction went on for about a week or so. I had gotten used to the dog being there. One morning I came out of my house, locked the door, and looked for the dog as I walked. I did not see him, but I walked anyway wondering where he was this particular morning. As I noticed, there was a man walking on the opposite side of the street slightly behind me. His pace was in keeping with mine; he was not trying to pass me. As he crossed the street behind me, once again, a familiar enemy showed up. Yes, you got it - fear!!! Where is my protection when I really need him? I kept walking and I looked back, and the person was still walking behind me. Just as I neared the vacant building that the dog would always depart from, there he was running towards me.

He had never done anything but walk before me and meet me at the bus stop, but this time he ran and

Encounter Five . . . Protected by Man's Best Friend

rubbed up against me and encircled me three times while I was walking. He did not leave me, but he walked side by side with me until I got to the corner and crossed the street. He stood right next to me, very closely. The person walked near us and looked at me as he passed by. The dog stood there, as usual, until I got on the bus.

The next day when it was time to catch the bus, there was no dog again. But what I noticed was a lady and her daughter coming out of her house a few steps before I arrived. We spoke and she and I began to walk in the same direction. She asked me where the bus stop was, and I told her I was on my way to it. We walked together and talked and did so every morning after that. You know what, I didn't see that dog any more after the last time he walked me to the bus stop and didn't leave my side. Once again, thank you God for My Angel to My Rescue by way of "man's best friend—the dog."

PONDER THIS

"A hand touched me and set me trembling on my hands and knees. He said, "Daniel, you who are highly esteemed, consider carefully the words I am about to speak to you, and stand up for I have now been sent to you." And when he said this to me, I stood up trembling." Daniel 10:10-11 People of God, understand that we are beloved of God and He wants us to know that He hears his children whenever we seek Him for help or any other request. He sends His angels to minister to us and on behalf of us. I asked Him every morning for His protection for me and others, but when He sent it, the protection was not presented in the form I was expecting, so I allowed fear to come in. However, God, in all His infinite wisdom, does not have to fit in our cookie-cutter mentality of how we think He should do things for us. He told me just as He told Daniel, *"Do not be afraid, Daniel (Roberta). Since the first day that you set your mind to gain understanding and to humble yourself before your God, your words were heard, and I (the angel) have come in response to them." Daniel 10:12*

Encounter Five . . . Protected by Man's Best Friend

Fear has no place in your mind or heart. Don't allow the enemy to rent space in your mind because he can't afford to pay the rent!!! You have BOSS status over fear and you will not allow fear to live in your soul!!! Courage, courage, courage!!! Sometimes the enemy comes at us like a flood and we become overwhelmed, fearful, etc., but be reminded when these circumstances come our way that the scripture says in *Isaiah 59:19b, "When the enemy shall come in like a flood, The Spirit of the Lord shall lift up a standard against him."* **(KJV)** That standard is the Word of God and it acts as a banner over us, waving the victory on our behalf. When the standard is lifted against us, we are able to speak the Word, *"For God hath not given us the spirit of fear; but of power, and of love, and of a sound mind." 2 Timothy 1:7* **(KJV)**

We must also be reminded not to worry about fear and any attacks from the enemy because *Deuteronomy 28:7 says, "The Lord will grant that the enemies who rise up against you will be defeated before you. They will come at you from one direction but flee from you*

in seven. But the LORD will help you win the battle over them. Hallelujah!!!

PRAYER

Father God, thank You for hearing my prayers, not because they are so great or magnificent, but because when You hear them, You send an answer, and for that I truly thank You. Lord help me to walk worthy of Your love and blessings that You bestow upon me. Thank You, Father, that You call us friend. Thank You for allowing us to know that You love us so much that the angels wonder, "What is man that You love us so!" Thank You for being our protector and a way out of no way. Jehovah, I love You. Amen.

Encounter Six...
Five Shiny Quarters

> *"Be not forgetful to entertain strangers: for thereby some have entertained angels unawares."*
> Hebrews 13:2 (KJV)

This encounter started just because I was hungry. I had a special male friend who had picked me up from work and brought me home. When we got inside the house, I noticed he had bought himself something to eat prior to picking me up, but didn't get anything for me. I was very upset and "hangry" (hungry+angry). He asked if he could eat his food first while it was hot, and he would go get me something as soon as he was done. The right thing for me to do would have been to agree to allow him to go ahead and eat, then go and get me something when he finished, but it seems, I was not having that. The truth of the matter, I felt, was friends buy friends a meal when they KNOW their friend is hungry and just getting off work. Oh well, he didn't see it that way!!!

However, I wouldn't allow him to eat in peace, so in anger he told me to come on let's go and get my food. I did just that!!! I got in the car without my purse, money, or anything else because he bought my food most of the time. As we were driving towards an area in the inner city to find something for me to eat, we got into an argument. This was not a great area to be in and I was not very familiar with it. Have you ever noticed some of the best "hole-in-the-wall" food joints are found in dives of neighborhoods? Anyway, to avoid further stirring this pot of anger from boiling over, I jumped out of the car when he approached a stop sign and began walking the opposite way of his driving. It was very dark, and the streets around me reeked with a feeling of evilness. I was walking and crying thinking to myself that was a stupid move, when I approached a bus stop where an older lady and a younger man were sitting on the bench. I excused myself to the lady and asked if she had 50 cents for me to make a phone call. She looked at me and smirked at me as if I was a menace to her. So, I turned to the man sitting there. I told him that a friend and I had an argument, and I had no money, but that I needed to call my daughter to come and get me.

This guy was a short, stubby white guy with a very friendly face, who said, "I don't have any money, but let's go and look in this pay phone behind this bus booth to see if there may be a quarter in there." *In my mind I was thinking, first of all, what is this white guy doing in this neighborhood, and secondly, there wouldn't be any money in there because in this area everybody, anybody, all bodies would have looked to see if any money was there.* And yes, this was during the time when pay phones were still on the street. OMG, not only did he pull out one quarter, but he pulled out five shiny quarters!!! In that dark, dreary area, the shiny quarters stood out like diamonds. I was so happy to see those quarters that I immediately held out my hand for two quarters, but he gave me all of them.

If I had been thinking, those five shiny quarters should have been a trigger to know that this was not

Encounter Six... Five Shiny Quarters

going to be a regular night for me. After all, I had had many "Angel encounters" in life and I was familiar with their work as ministering angels. But I wasn't thinking like that. So, I placed the call to my daughter, and she was on her way. The kind man told me he was going to stay with me until my daughter arrived. I didn't notice at the time, but I was not even scared walking and talking with this stranger. Nonetheless, I somehow felt protected.

I suggested we walk from the bus stop towards the direction my daughter would be coming. While we were walking the guy asked me if that was my friend in that car. I began looking around to see what car he was referring to because I didn't see a car. He mentioned that a car had been following us since we began walking and he thought it was my friend. A few minutes later, I did see my friend's car. He didn't approach me, but stopped for a moment and then pulled off, never asking me to get back in the car. I wondered why he didn't. After all, he knew I was not in familiar territory and I didn't like the dark much at all. What the what? So, the stranger and I continued walking down the street, and I noticed my daughter. She had my niece in the car with her, and they were driving opposite of the way we were walking. I flagged them over. So, they turned around and pulled up alongside us. I was so excited about seeing them because I was too ready to get out of this area. With excitement of being rescued, without thought, I began to quickly get into the car, but I paused and backed out of the car to turn to acknowledge and say thank you to the stranger who had stayed with me for the last hour. To my surprise, when I turned around, he was gone. Where did he go? My daughter asked me what I was looking at or what I was looking for.

I informed her I was looking for the stranger who stayed with me because I would like for her to take him where he wanted to go. I felt that was the least we could do for his kindness and protection. I looked across the street to see if I saw him walking and I didn't see him. We were in the middle of a block, so he could not have turned a corner. There was not a vacant lot for him to cross.

Encounter Six . . . Five Shiny Quarters

When I did get in the car, I asked my daughter and niece if they had seen the man who was walking with me when I flagged them over. They both said almost simultaneously, "No. I didn't see anybody with you." There was no way that they could have missed him because I was still talking to him, telling him that was my daughter in that car and that they were going to turn around. My daughter and niece did not see him, but I know he was there. HE WAS THERE!!! Of course, I never saw that stranger again.

I was still hungry, but I would exchange hunger for an eventful evening like that anytime, for I knew that was another episode of "Angels to My Rescue!" Again, all I can say is thank you Lord, for my "Angel to My Rescue."

PONDER THIS

During the times when you think things are too "dirty" for God to be a part of, invite Him in anyway. He will get down in the dirty with you. What does that mean? Sometimes we find ourselves in situations that we caused, but they turn out to be situations that God gets right in the middle of so that He can bring us out. This experience happened because I was "in my feelings" and I was trying to pick a fight. With that being said, God hung with me in this dirty.

There are so many of us who make some bad mistakes or decisions, or we take wrong directions in life that leaves us in places where we think what we have done is too bad for God to come and get us. What we don't remember is that God loves us from the gutter-most to the utter-most.

God pulls out all stops when it comes to rescuing His children. Don't let the enemy make you think you are too dirty and that He won't show up for you, because He's coming, just like a Father, if you are ready to come to Him.

Encounter Six . . . Five Shiny Quarters

I am reminded of a teaching from my Bishop about the two characteristics concerning "time," Chronos and Kairos. Just want to take a second to address the Kairos aspect. Kairos (used 86 times in the New Testament) refers to an opportune time, a "moment," or a "season" such as "harvest time." This is so important because when you are down and out, it seems you can't catch a break even if someone threw it to you. Or you are so far down in the dirty that you need a time designated and picked out just for you so that you can grab a hold of the lifeline and God can get your attention. During this time, He gives you a double portion of persistence, perseverance, stick-to-it-ness, along with whatever harvest of help you need. Kairos time doesn't last forever, but is appointed for a certain time. Ask God to give you a Kairos moment in your life so that He can bring you out of the "dirty."

During this particular time in my life, I wasn't doing everything I was supposed to do in my Christian walk, but I am a solid witness, when I got tired of being sick and tired, I asked God for a Kairos moment and He did just that for me. He brought me from that "dirty" and set me back on the track of following Him, and I have been going forth for Him ever since. Hallelujah!!!

PRAYER

Father God in the name of Jesus, there are times I am not strong enough to overcome some of the attacks of the enemy and I need your help. My heart's desire is to serve you and only you. My heart's desire is also to please you. Please provide me a Kairos moment so that I can come out of my "dirty." I thank you for not turning your back on me when I could not look confidently at you because of the place I was in. I need you God. Allow the spirit of repentance to take over my heart right now and renew the right spirit within me. Lord, I shall forever give you the praise. Amen.

Encounter Seven...
A Strange Place for Elevation

> *"But after he had considered this, an angel of the Lord appeared to him in a dream and said, "Joseph son of David, do not be afraid to take Mary home as your wife, because what is conceived in her is from the Holy Spirit. She will give birth to a son, and you are to give him the name Jesus, because he will save his people from their sins."' Matthew 1:20-21*

In my mind's eye, this encounter was a test of elevation to conquer my fear of the spiritual unknown and an effort to increase my faith. I always knew just as sure as there were godly angels, there were demons as well. I was scared of anything dark and evil and would not, could not face the idea of casting out demons as the scripture tells us. I wanted no part of these demons, or anything of that world. But, if I had not understood that God had given me power over the

Encounter Seven . . . A Strange Place for Elevation

power of the enemy, I would always be defeated by my fear to put the devil under my feet where he belongs.

So, thus begins this encounter. I used to own a big 10,000 square feet corner property with various living quarters in North St. Louis City, but I sold it to my best friend. At a point in my life, it was necessary for me to move back into this property for a short time, not because I wanted to, but circumstances caused me to have to. But at the time, I was the only one living in the building. Even though I needed to be here, I felt like this was a backwards move for me. I used to own this building, but now I must come back to it under a new owner. No matter how short of tenure it was, this was depressing to me.

One day while waiting for the local bus to take me home, I saw an Evangelist that I knew. I had not seen her in quite a while because she had moved out of town. We greeted each other in love, and she offered to take me home. I told her I didn't live very far from there, as a matter of fact, just around the corner from the church where we both attended. She would not have it (me catching the bus). She said she would take me home, so I accepted the ride. When we reached my home, Evangelist Lowe told me she had a word to give me from the Lord. Mind you, I had not seen Evangelist Lowe for several years, *but she had a word for me?* She proceeded to pause a little, as if she didn't know exactly what God was telling her to tell me, but at the same time began to speak what was being put in her mouth. Did you understand that?

At any rate, as we sat outside in the car, she began to say that God is saying that your current place of residence is a place of spiritual elevation, which was contrary to the fact that you think of it as a downgrade or demotion of some sort. She mentioned God wanted to teach me some things and that, though it would seem hard to me, I would be successful in learning. She mentioned that any test of the unknown would be hard, but with the instruction given from God, I would be able to pass this feat. She said she couldn't give me any other details but that was the message the Lord wanted her to deliver to me. How could she know? I was confused with some of this news, so as soon as I

Encounter Seven . . . A Strange Place for Elevation

got upstairs, I went before God asking for some understanding in receiving this prophecy. Boy, did He not show me what the prophecy meant!!! OMG to the max!!! Elevation, could HE not have started me out with something less dramatic!!!

So, here I am on the first night I stayed in the building. Remember, I was alone in that huge building. I had not unpacked many things, but my TV was set up and furniture was there. I borrowed a small bed that was left there and I washed it down good and put clean bedding on it before I left out earlier. I also left the TV on, and set out a lamp so I could see later that night when I returned home. So along with the light from the TV, I wasn't afraid to be in the building alone, because I used to own it and was familiar with it. However, I had never experienced what I am about to share with you.

I prayed over the house and blessed it by anointing each door entry and window by putting crosses on them with blessed oil. I remembered some sounds from before when I used to live there with my two children. But I wasn't scared then. That night I went to sleep with the television on. Sometime in the middle of the night I was awakened by the movement of my bed. I woke up but thought I was dreaming so I went back to sleep. It seemed like approximately 15 minutes passed by and I was awakened again to this very violent shaking of the bed. This time I knew I wasn't dreaming. Lord, oh Lord, was I afraid!!! I noticed it was pitch black and the television was no longer on. The bed had stopped shaking, but I was still shaking. I jumped out of it to reach for the lamp, praying that it had a light bulb in it. Thank God it did!

I was afraid to go back to sleep and couldn't go anywhere because it was in the middle of the night, and I didn't have a car at the time. All night until daybreak, I heard the eerie squeaking of plastic like you hear in a horror movie. I thought I was going to have a heart attack. Over the next couple of nights, it was more of the same actions along with other sounds of shutting doors, all electricity going off on my floor, footsteps walking on the floor during all times of the night, foul smelling odors appearing right before these other acts took place, and so much more. Of all of the

Encounter Seven . . . A Strange Place for Elevation

things that did happen, most of which I won't go into detail about, there is one thing I would like to mention in detail that really propelled me into motivation to attain this new level of faith.

Yay! I would get a reprieve because I had to go to Colorado for a week to attend a training class for a nationwide service company designed to alleviate poverty. This class was to help me get ready for an assignment with them. Once there, I was able to get some sound sleep. Also, this was an opportunity to pray during my off time, and I began wrapping my mind around hearing from God and getting this "growth party" started.

Once I got home, it didn't take long for my little "pesky friends" to show up again. However, God began by feeding me scriptures on being a conqueror through Christ Jesus and that He didn't give me a spirit of fear and many, many more scriptures. At nighttime, I would watch a TV program that showed scriptures with beautiful nature backgrounds on a Christian-based television channel. As time went on, I became stronger in my walk, my words, my faith, and overall, stronger in obeying God. I was eating the Word of God everywhere I went, throughout the day and night.

My grandson, Jeriah, loved to come and visit his granny, and one weekend he came to stay with me. It was customary for me to spoil him as if he was a little king when he was over. I did things that any grandparent would do to make their little ones happy. I prepared his favorite foods, had his favorite snacks on hand, planned activities like building tents to watch movies, etc. No matter what he was doing, he would always come find me to see what I was doing. However, this particular weekend was different. Jeriah was watching TV for like five straight hours. I thought he had dozed off, so I went into his room to see if he was ok. When I walked in, he was wrapped up in the cover as if he was afraid of something. It turns out that something had frightened him. He asked me, "Who was that man with the glasses staring at you while you were studying your Bible in the kitchen?" I told him he must have seen the reflection of something on the television. He got up out of the bed and followed me

Encounter Seven . . . A Strange Place for Elevation

everywhere I went in the house until it was time for bed.

Jeriah must have seen this figure more times after this weekend because when he would come over, he would not be left alone in any room without me. Now, the inner person of me—the spirit person felt, *devil, it is one thing to mess with me, but now you have gone too far, you want to bother my grandson? Father God today!!! Please teach me what I need to know and do in order to overcome my fears and believe that I do have power over the enemy.* It was really on now!!! I was up for the challenge.

So, that night when I went to sleep, the angel of the Lord appeared to me in a dream. In my dream, he was dressed in a long white robe, had huge wings, a face that looked like an ordinary man, and he was surrounded by a very bright light. He announced himself by name and said he was a messenger sent from God. Of course, you know it, I cannot remember the name he said, and I can just kick myself for subconsciously not paying more attention to this dream then! As if I had control over this, right!!! The angel continued by saying, "I have a message for you. As I was with Moses, so I will be with you; I will never leave you nor forsake you. Be strong and courageous. Be strong and very courageous. Be careful to obey all the law. Do not turn from it to the right or to the left, that you may be successful wherever you go." He disappeared after saying that or I must have started to dream something else.

In the morning when I rose, I began searching for those scriptures in the Bible and I found it in Joshua 1:5-7. These scriptures became my spiritual breakfast, lunch and dinner; along with other scriptures that taught me how to fight fear and those that increased my faith in God for I was more than a conqueror. I spoke with my Pastor, the Bishop Anthony L. Taylor, Sr., and shared some of the things that had been happening to me. I asked him for guidance in dealing with this experience, but he told me he had not experienced this before. He advised me to continue to read and study those and other scriptures to increase my faith in God. It took some time, but God got me to the point of quoting scriptures, actually eating

Encounter Seven . . . A Strange Place for Elevation

scriptures as if they were some kind of superhero power capsules, which gave me feelings of spiritual confidence that God was in control, and that He had given me what I needed to pass this test.

I remained in the building for a while longer, but I noticed I was no longer scared, and that my language was changing. I was now speaking and believing I was the head and not the tail. I believed that greater was He that was within me than He that was in the world. I now believed that I was more than a conqueror through Christ Jesus. Now at the bus stop, I was thanking God and confessing power over the enemy of fear; walking home I was thanking God for my stable mind, and I could ask for what I wanted and believe I could receive it. Wow, haven't you ever had a period in your Christian life when you were totally on fire for God with His Word as your weapon of destruction? At that time, if I have to say so for myself, I was a walking fireball. Not bragging, this was just my true perception of myself during this difficult time of a new level.

As I armed myself more and more with God's Word, I thanked God for Christian programs. I was finally able to conquer a new level of fear, but what I really hold dear is "for I am convinced that neither death, nor life, nor angels, nor principalities, nor things present, nor things to come, nor powers, nor height, nor depth, nor any other created thing, will be able to separate me from the love of God, which is in Christ Jesus our Lord." Romans 8:38-39

Although, I did live in this building a while longer, I did take control over my fear and gained control over my dwelling space. With the help of God and my angel, I thank Him once again for His Messenger, another "Angel to My Rescue."

PONDER THIS

When people see God's anointing on a person's life, they often want that same anointing, but they don't know what it took to get that anointing. Most often they don't want to live the sacrifice required to receive the anointing. Elevation of any sort in God's kingdom requires a sold-out mind and spirit.

After everything I went through during this elevation, God did not leave me at any time. If you

Encounter Seven ... A Strange Place for Elevation

want to be used by God, you have to give Him all of you, and He will mold you like a potter does with clay. This was very hard for me during the molding process, but I learned to trust God in my heart in a way that I can't really explain.

God looks for those who will allow Him to elevate them. And when He does find you, there is nothing more beautiful than the feet of those following God. Salvation is free but at the same time it costs you to follow Him—your life.

Encounter Eight...
You Gotta Bless Me

> *"I will not let you go unless you bless me!"* Genesis 32:26

Just as Jacob wrestled with focused intent to receive his blessing from the Angel, I believe I experienced pretty much that same intensity concerning a situation that I needed God's attention on. Now, the hardest part of telling this encounter is because it happened at a time in my life that I didn't listen to God as I should have—this I know.

SO, CHECK THIS OUT...

I met a man through a well-known and highly publicized dating service; I'll call him "Q." After talking on the phone for over three weeks, I felt I knew Q somewhat and was comfortable with our conversations. He didn't disrespect me, nor did he use

Encounter Eight... You Gotta Bless Me

too many "four-letter" words. We finally decided to meet at a public place, which was located between my house and his. If you have ever been on a blind date, you can understand the "butterflies in the stomach" caused by those feelings of nervous anticipation. That was me.

When we met in person, we didn't have any problems keeping a conversation going between us. Q was everything my nature liked, tall, dark, and I thought handsome, with a great body. You could tell he worked out and was very physically fit. I started mentally going over my checklist. Check One off the list, he met my physical expectations. However, Q was also a few years my junior, but I could handle that. I was elated to know his mother was a Pastor and he appeared to understand Jesus as his Savior. Of course, thank you, God, right?! So, I said Check Two off the list, for him being a great conversationalist and a little funny also! Q wasn't working a "BIG" job at the time because he said he was receiving disability and had received a large settlement of some sort. Check Three off the list, for him being financially secure. At that time, I didn't ask what the disability was, didn't really matter, so I thought anyway. Apparently, he felt equally pleased with me physically and mentally, plus I had a decent job.

Q called me to see if I made it home after our date, and called every day after that. When I finally invited him over to my house for dinner, he asked if I had a photo album of me. I gave him the album and returned to the kitchen to finish preparing our dinner. He later asked if I had a pair of scissors, which I gave him. After dinner and after he left, I grabbed the photo album to put it away only to find he had gone through the whole album and cut out the heads of any guy I was on the picture with. **First flag, right!!!** No, I thought it was cute. Oh, he was jealous already and wanted me totally to himself. What was I thinking? This was the beginning of a seven-year tumultuous relationship. After this incident, there were many more flags that I chose to ignore because I wanted what I wanted even when I found out that it was not God's will for me. So now that I have said that, no judging is allowed throughout this encounter, so here goes:

Encounter Eight... You Gotta Bless Me

Flag 2 - One day Q and I were watching TV, and out of the blue, my 12-year-old son came by, stood and looked at my friend for what seemed like eternity, but was only about five seconds or so. What came out of my son's mouth bothered me because he said, "Momma, he's gone fool around and kill our family." Who says that, especially right in the face of the accused? I should have thought, flag number two, but instead I chose to tell my son, "Boy, you are being silly, get out of here." He left out but that saying never left my mind.

Flag 3 - During this time, he was with me all the time and rarely did I get a chance to be with family or friends. He tried every chance he got to alienate me from them. When one of my favorite nieces was getting married (all my nieces are favorites), he held me hostage, literally, and I could not attend her wedding. I don't think I ever told her or any of my family what happened. At this point I tried breaking this relationship off because I was beginning to see the real man. Q called me every day for about a month leaving messages saying how much he missed me, how sorry he was to make me upset, and how he didn't want to live without me. Yes, you got the picture, all of those things.

Flag 4 - I got a call one morning, about 2:00 a.m., from a close friend, who told me Q showed up at her house threatening to kill her and her daughters if she didn't convince me to come back to him. She also said he had a gun!!! This is when I found out he went through my phone and got every family and friend's phone number. I phoned Q trying to ask him what was going on and he proceeded to beg me if he could come see me, that he needed to talk with me. He came, and we became friends again. I told myself it was because I didn't want him to hurt any family and friends, especially knowing he had access to their addresses and phone numbers.

Flag 5 - One evening when my daughter came home from work, she discovered she could not get the key to work in the main entrance door she used to get into her

Encounter Eight ... You Gotta Bless Me

apartment. After trying to get into that part of the apartment building unsuccessfully, she went around to the front of the building where she was able to gain access to her apartment entrance. But as she was opening her door, she noticed Q standing there in an open doorway opposite of her door. It startled her and when she looked at him, she had a feeling he might be up to no good. You know the saying, "Keep your friends close, but keep your enemies closer." I thought that was what I needed to do in order to keep everyone safe around me.

Flag 6 - Many incidents began to happen more and more that made me know for sure that I had to get out of this relationship for good, but it was hard because I was concerned about people I loved and cared for. My play mother became ill and was hospitalized. I went to the hospital to see her one night not knowing that Q followed me, and saw me hug her son. Later Q asked me what I had done that evening, and I told him I visited a friend at the hospital. However, he was more interested in who the man was I embraced.

Inadvertently, I told him the guy's name. Soon after my friend mentioned some crazy man calls him daily threatening him. I then remembered Q had all my phone contacts. Q kept telling me if I left him, he would hurt a lot of people I loved and cared for. Unfortunately, I did not go back to the hospital, and was not there when my play mother died.

Flag 7 - One night he picked me up, said he wanted to go for a ride, and then get something to eat. He began to talk about how he wanted to be intimate with me because we hadn't been intimate for a long time. I didn't want to and was not interested! We were riding for about one and a half hours and ended up somewhere in unincorporated North County on dark swerving roads. He was very angry at this time because I refused his requests, and he kept saying I could kill you on this road and no one would know it and kept trying to get me to say something just so he could do something evil. I could tell, so I said nothing for about an hour. I was scared and I prayed that

Encounter Eight . . . You Gotta Bless Me

nothing would happen to me. I was familiar with portions of North County but not where we were. He pulled over and parked behind some shrubberies where his car could not be seen from the road and kept cursing and telling me I was going to die right there. But I kept pleading the blood of Jesus and asking for a way out. Suddenly, after about thirty minutes of ranting, he began driving again until we reached a major street in North County and stopped at a stop sign. That's when I jumped out of the car and ran into an opened place of business. I asked if I could make a local phone call, and the retailer allowed me to use his phone. I called my friend, Evone, and asked her to pick me up when I found out from the retailer where I was. She came. Thank God for Evone! She went through so much with me and this man! She probably judged me on a few occasions, but never refused to help me.

Flag 8 - I later found out he had cameras all over my house and could see everything that happened in my house. One day a male friend (just a friend) of mine came over, who needed to lay his head in a peaceful place for about an hour. So, I told him to go ahead and lay across my bed for a short time. Q was at work about this time, so I didn't really worry about any confrontation. When he awakened, he thanked me, we talked for a few minutes, and he was on his way.

That very next day Q brought me a beautiful teddy bear and told me to sit it on the chest of drawers which was sitting directly opposite of the bed. I did as he requested. This way, he said, you will be able to think about me whenever you open your eyes and see this teddy bear. I never knew what version of Q I was going to see during the day. Sometimes he was loving, other times he was moody, sometimes he wanted to be bothered, and other times he didn't, etc.

Later that day we got into a big argument about something, and I took the teddy bear and threw it away because I was very angry. Within an hour or so Q called and made small talk. He then asked if I had looked at the teddy bear anymore today. I told him, no, because I was mad at him. He began to ask questions like did I move the teddy bear, where had I placed it,

Encounter Eight... You Gotta Bless Me

or did I put something in front of it, or a piece of clothing on top of it.

As I thought, I remembered at one time Q didn't think my coffee drinking was healthy and he wanted me to quit drinking it. I told him I would stop, with intentions to do so. But one day I found some coffee on sale and wanted to try it. I bought it and sat it on the kitchen table. When I talked to Q, he asked, "Are you still drinking coffee?" I said no because I had not had an opportunity to even open the box. He said, "Are you trying a new kind, and I thought you were going to stop." He talked enough about this coffee to let me know he sees it.

I later put two and two together only to realize there must have been a camera in the teddy bear and when I threw it in the trash; he could not tell where the teddy bear was with what he was viewing on his footage. He just knew something was obstructing his view. I asked a friend of mine who was an electrician how I could find out if there were cameras installed anywhere in my house and he told me some things to look for. I asked if he could come by and help me look and he did. By the time we were able to look, we found many camera cords remaining from where Q had disconnected cameras. Just think, if Q had given me that teddy bear the day before when my friend came by and laid across my bed, there is no doubt in my mind I would have been a dead woman. I wouldn't have known there was a camera inside of the teddy bear and here I was helping another man lay comfortably in my bed, even though he was just a friend. Whew, a bullet that I dodged. Thank you, God.

Flag 9 - One night when we were out riding with Q behind the wheel, we were stopped by a male and female cop. The male officer asked Q to get out of the car, show license and that whole routine. It was discovered that Q had a warrant for his arrest. While the male officer was handling Q, the female officer asked me to get out of the car. She asked what the relationship was between me and Q. I told her he was my friend. She then asked whose car it was, and I told her mine. She began to tell me, "Lady, you seem nice

Encounter Eight . . . You Gotta Bless Me

enough and I see a Bible in the back seat of your car. You should get as far away from this man as you can. If he brings harm to you, there's not much going to be done about it because he's very mentally ill, and has a very long record of things he has done. He's bi-polar, schizophrenic, and borderline personality disorder all wrapped up inside." She told me other things that shook me to the core. I had been praying to God for my release without anyone getting hurt, but it was at that time, after that conversation with that female officer that made me feel the intensity of demonstrating to God, if you don't bless me, I can't and won't let go of you.

By now I knew beyond a shadow of doubt that it was time to get out of this tangled web I had weaved for myself. I began to cry in anguish, pray, read God's Word, and fall prostrate on the floor seeking Him for the plan of my deliverance. One late night in prayer, because there was no sleeping or time for peace, I was in total torment and needed to hear from God! During this seven-year period, I was still attending church regularly, still praying and living a "decent" Christian life, but not in right standing with God.

My Pastor had sat me down from ministry, and any positions I held in the church, and encouraged me to return to holy and righteous living. Because I had not let go of my faith and kept a repenting heart no matter what may have been happening in my life, God did not turn His back on me. Late one night during prayer meeting, Pastor brought Mother Williams to me and told me to go and talk to her and share my experience with her. God, oh my God, I don't want anyone to really know what I've been through. Nevertheless, at your word I will do it. I went and spoke with Mother Williams, and she listened to what I had to say very intently without a word of interruption. After I was finished confessing, she told me, "We are going to fast and pray together, and believe God for your deliverance."

A few other things happened before my deliverance. Mother Williams and I were still very much in prayer and fasting and I was still crying out in anguish for God's help and deliverance. In the

Encounter Eight . . . You Gotta Bless Me

meantime, I purchased a house because I was going to use my building for business purposes only. Still praying and believing for deliverance, Q would come to the new house and help me work on it from time to time. Over time I did complete the house and moved in. Q knew something was changing about me, but didn't know what. He had no idea that an all-out attack was being set up against him.

My Pastor had been teaching us about sending our angels forth for work and ministering on our behalf. He also taught about how all of God's children had angels to help us fight our battles. Our angels would go before us conquering and slaying the work of the enemy. Oh my, oh my, I didn't know how close my deliverance was.

On Thanksgiving 2007, I was awakened around 7:00 a.m., by a knock on the door. I got up to answer, and it was Q. I let him in and asked if everything was okay. He asked me if I was cooking for Thanksgiving and I told him no, that I was going over to my daughter's. I went and got back in the bed. He was walking through the house cursing loudly and saying things like I should have stayed where I was, and could have gotten any meal I wanted. But no, I come back here to you and you didn't cook nothing. The more he talked, the angrier he got. At one point he came and stood on the side of the bed where I was and had his fist clenched and a look as if he wanted to hit me. I looked at him, this time without fear. I heard the voice of the Lord clearly say to me, "This is the day of your deliverance." I sat up in the bed, swung my legs out of the bed, and stood up right beside Q. I didn't look at him and hardly acknowledged him. I proceeded to put on my blue jogging suit laying on the chair at the foot of my bed from the day before and my tennis shoes which were sitting right in front of the chair. I walked out of the bedroom to the vestibule by the front door and I stood there with the door opened and waited for him to walk towards the front.

When he did, he came with a lot of lip, still cussing, and angry. I looked at him and none of that phased me. There was a soldier's spirit that stood up on the inside of me. There was no fear and I was ready to conquer whatever lay before me. He continued to

Encounter Eight... You Gotta Bless Me

curse me, and I asked him, "Are you done, because I am tired of hearing it? Make your move or shut up." That angered him more than I could tell you and he balled his big, strong fist, and raised his hand as if to get ready to lay me out. He was 6'2" and solid, so if connection was made, I would have been hurt. Just as he lifted his arm and drew back, we both heard this loud noise as if it were a big book falling on a wooden floor. Q looked startled and looked around as if someone else was back there. I heard the noise also, but never moved, and of a truth, I was not scared even now. He lowered his hand and began accusing me of having a man hidden back in the bedroom. Once again, because no one came forward and he wasn't going back there, the more he accused, the madder he got. He clenched his fist once again and raised his hand to hit me, and we heard that same loud sound as if it was a big book falling to the wooden floor.

I heard it again and wondered within myself what the noise was because every room in my house was carpeted except for the kitchen and the vestibule. A book hitting carpet does not sound that loud coming from any other room in this house. As I stood by the door listening to him, I said for the last time, "You need to leave me, my family and loved ones alone. I am no longer afraid of you and my angels are here to fight my battle, so if you need to make a move, you need to go ahead and do it, otherwise leave and don't ever darken any door of mine ever again." I notice I said that with power and authority and with conviction as if I owned those words!! Hallelujah!!!

When I looked out the door, to my surprise, there were my next-door neighbors, which were four young men that I called out to and spoke and asked if they could come here and they did. When they came up the stairs, they asked if everything was okay because the look on Q's face told the story. I looked at Q and said, "No, he was just leaving." I made small talk with my neighbors and they went on next door. Q walked out the door and I didn't see him for many years, until one day I saw him at the bus stop.

For seven years I had grown weary of trying to get out of his life and keep him out of mine. It seemed every other day we were breaking up and I was just

Encounter Eight . . . You Gotta Bless Me

tired. I now understood how women—strong minded women, could be reduced to this type of behavior and mental abuse. He never physically harmed me, but I was a mental mess. Those on the outside looking in, now as some of you read this, and then, when others found out what I was going through, wondered how and why I didn't just walk away. This was a long experience, but I thank God with everything in me for sending an angel to my rescue once again. This time, I wasn't going to let go until God blessed me! Hallelujah!!!

Encounter Nine...
I Was Preparing to Die Until He Spoke Life into Me

> *"I will not die but live and will proclaim what the LORD has done for me."* Psalm 118:17

"Ms. Collier, you will need someone here with you tomorrow morning before we are able to perform the surgery. Have you contacted anyone yet?"

This was the question I was asked when I went to the hospital as a result of my Primary Care Physician telling me to go directly to the hospital after a routine doctor's visit. Well, let me backup and start with how I came to that question.

I first must let you know, during this time in my life, I was under a doctor's care for a number of medical conditions. I had gone for a scheduled appointment for health status. My appointment was early in the morning and I was instructed to go and

Encounter Nine . . . I Was Preparing to Die Until He Spoke Life into Me

take a blood test. I did so and upon completion of the visit, my doctor refilled my prescriptions and told me she would call me if there were any unusual outcomes from the blood test. I made my next three-month appointment and said okay.

During the day, I received two or three calls from the doctor's office, but I didn't answer them because I thought they were calls to let me know my prescriptions were ready to pick up. Later that evening when I was checking my messages, I found that these calls were urgent messages to contact my doctor's office. By the time I got the messages, the doctor's office was closed, and I had to call the exchange. I did, and the doctor on call told me to go directly to the hospital; they were expecting me. I explained I couldn't go at that minute, because I was waiting for my daughter to pick up her son from my house. The doctor told me to go to the hospital emergency as soon as I could. He never told me what was wrong, other than there were some abnormalities in my blood test.

After my grandson left, I went to the Emergency Room, which was not far at all from where I lived. As the doctor had said, they were awaiting my arrival. While I was standing there answering questions from the triage nurse, she suddenly had to step away for a second. There was a man sitting right next to where I was standing. He began to try to flirt with me. I'm sorry, I am generally not a woman who judges a book by its cover, but this fellow was not my cup of tea in any stretch of anybody's imagination.

He could have been decently attractive if I was able to see through the terribly unkempt facial hair; if he didn't smell like alcohol every time he opened his mouth, and he kept smiling with at least three teeth missing out of his mouth. However, I spoke to him when he spoke to me, and was very glad when the nurse returned to help me. Well, if you have been to the Emergency Room lately, you know usually there is a long waiting period, unless of course, you are already practically dead. To my surprise, they immediately sent me in for vitals and some more blood samples.

Encounter Nine . . . I was Preparing to Die Until He Spoke Life into Me

Guess who was right next to me in the same room having vitals and blood drawn. You guessed it!!! Mr. no teeth, smelling like alcohol, but still smiling man from the Registration Desk. So, he is still trying to flirt, and the nurses were trying to get him to pay attention to them. I finished before he did, and they asked me to sit in the waiting room until my name was called. I immediately said okay and went and found a seat in the back of the room. This hospital's Emergency Room was **ALWAYS** full and busy. I thought for sure I had escaped my new best friend.

As I sat there wondering why I was there, because I still had not been given any clue as to why, I went back up to the Registration Desk to ask why I had to come to the ER in such a hurry. What was wrong? I felt absolutely fine!!! I was told my kidneys were showing some serious problems and that I had to be checked out. I went back to my seat thinking about how and why my kidneys were showing problems. So, I had not been seated for more than sixty seconds, when my new best friend came and sat right next to me. Being somewhat annoyed, but still respectable, I listened as he chattered on and on. After taking me through a Bible question and answer session for about 55 minutes, I must have passed his test. He told me he was going to stop playing around and do what he was there to do. He also told me he wasn't there for himself, but that God sends him to the ER to deliver messages to people and sometimes pray for them. Yeah, right! At least, so I thought, *God sent you to give me a message.* So, I asked him, "Okay, what's the message?"

He said, "I don't know you and don't think I have ever seen you in my life, but God told me to tell you, "QUIT PREPARING TO DIE! IT IS NOT YOUR TIME YET! THERE IS STILL MORE LIVING TO DO FOR YOU. THERE ARE MORE LIVES HE WANTS TO TOUCH THROUGH YOU. HE SAYS HE HAS INVESTED TOO MUCH IN YOU TO TAKE YOU NOW." There were many other things he said to me that evening, but I have to admit, somehow his body odor, bad breath, no teeth, unkempt facial air,

Encounter Nine . . . I Was Preparing to Die Until He Spoke Life into Me

etc., no longer mattered to me because the voice of God had spoken to me through this man.

He was 100% accurate in the things he said. I was going through a tough battle with my heart, because I had had a heart attack and the left muscles of the heart were left very weak. So, I was told my heart was too weak to perform surgery to implant a defibrillator or pacemaker. (This whole section of my life and how God took me through will be shared through another book.) After he finished delivering what God gave him to speak to me, I could see what looked like a drained spirit come over his face. That playful, smiling spirit seemed to have disappeared. He told me he was tired and going home. He also said he was hungry. He didn't ask me for money, but I did give him enough money to get him something to eat.

The things he shared with me were things only God knew about. Yes, I had been planning my funeral, writing my obituary, and preparing for all things heading in the direction of my homegoing. Just as quickly as he entered my presence, he was gone. I was admitted into the hospital that night with the report of having stage four kidney failure. The first thing I was told by the admitting doctor was, based on my test results; I was going to have to start dialysis. Why? I asked. I feel just fine, and I told the doctor the same. She began to ask me questions like, "Can you still urinate?" "Yes, with no problem." "Have you had a bowel movement?" "Yes, just before I came to the hospital." "Does your back hurt?" "No."

They decided to keep me while still trying to convince me I needed to go on dialysis which I refused. Despite what the blood tests were showing, all functions of the kidney were still being performed adequately, and I saw no reason to interject dialysis where it was not needed. I began at that point to speak healing over my kidneys.

While I was there, I did develop chest pains, and the focus switched from my kidneys to my heart. They did an MRI of the heart and later that evening told me, based on the results from the MRI, I needed emergency surgery because there was a large amount of blockage visible. The team of doctors showed me

Encounter Nine . . . I Was Preparing to Die Until He Spoke Life into Me

the x-rays with large spots known to them as the blockage. They knew surgery was necessary, but was not sure what they would find once they opened me up. They scheduled the surgery for about 6:30 a.m., and told me it was imperative to have someone there with me just in case it was necessary to make some decisions.

I was not in the habit of giving my family and friends a report every time I went to the doctor. I only told them when I felt it was necessary. Less stress on them thinking the worst and less stress on me having to know how stressed they were thinking about me. I had a mother who had passed a few years earlier with all the conditions I was now experiencing.

However, thinking about who I would contact to be with me during surgery, of course my daughter came to my mind. But LaTonya had just started a new job, and I didn't want her to miss work already. So, I didn't call her. I thought about Sis. Pat, a dear friend of mine who was like a sister to me, one who would do anything she could to help me; yet she had obligations with her mother and grandchildren. I then thought about my sister, Shawna, who also was new on a job and decided not to ask her.

All things and all persons considered; I decided the one I really needed to be there with me was my father. I prayed right then and thanked God for His healing. When the nurse asked me that evening who was coming to be with me in the morning, I told her my father was going to be there. She said okay and reiterated the importance of this surgery and that my father needed to be at the hospital by 5:45 a.m., to make sure he was properly registered and informed of his potential duties prior to surgery.

Moving forward to the next morning, they came about 5:00 a.m., to prep me for my heart surgery, and the nurse asked me if I had contacted my father to tell him the time and location. I assured her that I had. By 5:45 a.m., there was no visible sign of my father; by 6:15 no sign. By 6:30 a.m., they had to go ahead and start the surgery. Once again, I assured them he was at

Encounter Nine . . . I Was Preparing to Die Until He Spoke Life into Me

the hospital and he would be there when they needed him.

They placed me on this long, narrow, not-so-comfortable metal bed, and strapped my arms away from my body. The surgery was taking place through my left arm up to my heart. They recognized I had atrial fibrillation, and that meant they could not put me under total sedation, but enough to keep me from feeling anything but minor pressure.

Once the surgeon was suited and began inserting the medical tools in my arm through open ports, I remembered there was also a camera inserted that allowed the surgeon to see what he was doing. A few minutes into the surgery, I heard the doctor say "Stop!" I felt the uncertainty in the atmosphere as to why he was stopping the procedure so abruptly. He soon stated there was no blockage.

One of the operating nurses who prepped me that morning for surgery, joined me in a word of prayer prior to taking me to the surgery room. She leaned over and whispered in my ear, "I guess your Father showed up after all!" That He did! That He did! Hallelujah!!

I was put in recovery for a period and then taken back to my room. I talked to Sis. Pat sometime during the day and told her about the surgery. Later that evening, she, and Mother Williams came to the hospital to see me. While they were there, the team of doctors came in befuddled as to what happened earlier. They were prepared to show me the x-rays with the blockage and explain why surgery was necessary. In the midst of them beginning to try to explain what could have happened, I just told them, "No explanation necessary, **My Father** just showed up as I promised He would."

I was grateful to have Sis. Pat and Mother Williams as witnesses that God did just what I asked Him to do, and the doctors were even dumbfounded as to what had happened. It's been at least two years since this has happened. Once again, I thank God for more "Angels to My Rescue." This time by: 1) My new best friend delivering a message from the Lord;

Encounter Nine . . . I Was Preparing to Die Until He Spoke Life Into Me

and 2) the angels showing up to cancel the blockage right before the doctor's eyes. **Won't He Do It!!!**

PONDER THIS

I didn't die. I lived!!! And now I'm telling the world what GOD did. GOD tested me, He pushed me hard, but He didn't hand me over to Death.

I Was Predestined

> *"Before I formed you in the womb, I knew you, before you were born, I set you apart." Jeremiah 1:5*

Before I put pen to paper to write this book, I sought counsel from God, even though I knew He was the one who told me to write the book in the first place. ***"For those God foreknew, he also predestined to be conformed to the image of his Son, that he might be the firstborn among many brothers and sisters." (Romans 8:29)***

I don't know why He chose me, but He did. He is still transforming me every day, whereof I am so thankful. I am sharing my encounters in hope that someone can be encouraged in knowing that God loves us so much, that He has given us every possible resource to assist us in living a successful Godly life. Angels are one of those resources.

God chose me, and thank God He prepared my heart to choose Him. He knew me before He put me in my mother's belly, just as He did you. He already had a plan for me to be used for His glory. He kept me because of His plan for me. *"For I know the plans I have for you," declares the LORD, "plans to prosper you and not to harm you, plans to give you hope and a future." (Jeremiah 29:11)*

God doesn't bless a mess in anyone's life, but what He does is find favor in us even before we fully know Him and His love; even before we are walking in total righteousness. He then guides us to and through the plan He has for us so that we can have an established end. That's called LOVE, topped with a healthy serving of the Favor of God! *"Surely, LORD, you bless the righteous; you surround them with your favor as with a shield." (Psalm 5:12)*

So, now that you have read some things in this book and you are on the fence about whether you can receive angelic assistance, just know that I was predestined for these experiences, and I am a changed woman every day because of Angels to My Rescue! Hallelujah!!!

About the Author

Roberta Collier is a first-time author and Minister of the Gospel of Jesus Christ. She is a native of St. Louis, Missouri, who has published her book titled, "Angels to My Rescue."

Roberta is made up of many things, but her most diligent aspect is all about God and His purpose for her life. She is on the Ministerial staff at New Hope Worship Center, where Apostle Anthony L. Taylor, Sr. is her Overseer. Roberta is also the Executive Director of Providers & More Professional Services, LLC., which helps provide event planning and administrative services to executives, businesses, and individuals in need. Roberta is an avid volunteer who has volunteered at many local businesses and churches. Roberta loves the institution of family, where she has a daughter and two grandsons. She lost her beloved son in 2015.

About the Author

Roberta is also currently working on a Christian-based game entitled "SLR According to Solomon." This game consists of topics about sex, love, and relationships adapted from the book of Solomon. SLR According to Solomon is a fun, enlightening way for married couples, and single people to openly learn and discuss topics that don't usually get discussed in a church setting.

Personal Encounter(s)

1. Write down a time(s) when you had an encounter with an angel(s).
2. What was your favorite part of the book?

I'd like to hear from you. Please email me at robertacollier01@gmail.com.

www.ingramcontent.com/pod-product-compliance
Lightning Source LLC
Chambersburg PA
CBHW071528080526
44588CB00011B/1600